-you are safe now

a poetry collection

jemima atar

This book is dedicated to

the younger me

This 1st edition published in Great
Britain in 2022 by Jemima Atar

Text © Jemima Atar 2022.
Illustrations © Juliana Lagerstedt 2022.

Jemima Atar asserts the moral right to be
identified as the author of this work.

A catalogue record of this book is
available from the British Library.

ISBN: 978-1-911443-15-5 (Paperback)
ISBN: 978-1-911443-16-2 (eBook)

Cover image by: Sarameeya Aree
Illustrations by: Julliana Lagerstedt
Book design by: SWATT Books Ltd

Jemima Atar's '*you are safe now*' is a poetry collection about the trauma of sexual abuse and its emotional, physical, and spiritual aftereffects. Based on a combination of her own personal experiences and those of many other survivors she has spoken to, the author explores complementary themes. These include losing childhood and reconnecting to the inner child, the loss of faith and the reclamation of faith in oneself, and the journey from powerlessness and voicelessness to self-definition and finding the confidence to speak out. Throughout the book, Jemima tells her own and others' stories through poems about suffering interspersed with poems about hope and healing, highlighting the non-linear nature of recovery, and how moments of growth can exist side-by-side with the hauntings of the past.

Trigger Warning:

Please note that this book contains explicit topics that some might find distressing, harmful, or triggering. Sensitive issues explored include: trauma, PTSD, rape, sexual abuse, physical abuse, emotional abuse, child abuse, violence, loss, suicide, self-harm, sexism/misogyny. Graphic imagery is also used. Please exercise discretion if you believe these issues may cause you distress. If you find yourself feeling overwhelmed in reaction to this content, please take time out to look after yourself, and know that there are resources to support you.

Samaritans: To talk about anything that is upsetting you, you can contact Samaritans 24 hours a day, 365 days a year.
Call 116 123 (free from any phone)
Website: www.samaritans.org

Nightline: If you're a student, you can visit the Nightline website to see if your university or college offers a night-time listening service.
Website: nightline.ac.uk

SHOUT: Shout 85258 is a free, confidential, 24/7 text-messaging support service for anyone who is struggling to cope.
Website: giveusashout.org

The Survivors Trust: Provides confidential information, advice and support for people who have experienced rape and sexual violence.
Free helpline: 08088 010818
Website: www.thesurvivorstrust.org

I am feeling
Years of hurt I vowed to never feel

– pain is a debt

Without
the dimension of time
two truths can
exist simultaneously.
I have the right to feel
both liberated
and abused

– holding both

I see you now and
I'm sorry
I had to leave you then.
We made it
You brave thing
and I am so proud of you

– conversations with
the younger me

The force
of you inside me
was so strong
It pushed me to a place
where I ignored the pain

– dissociation

Where was my voice
telling you to stop
maybe it was with my body
in the clouds
maybe the clouds
cushioned the fact
that I had to be silent
for you to stay

– floating

I am still hurting
from the first time.
I am hurting for the girl
who sat in her English class the next day
hurting

– branded

It was just us three
in my bed
you, me
and my pain

– where were you god

If I give you my body
I begged

will you promise not to take anyone else's?

– please don't cheat on me

How did you know
I wanted it
if you never asked me

      – consent requires
        a conversation

The bliss

of ignorance

does not exist

so that

you can shame yourself for it

years later

        – can't you see how

         beautiful defence

         mechanisms are

You squeezed
the vitality from
my identity
until you
had all the juice
and I was left
with the seeds

– i will plant myself
again someday

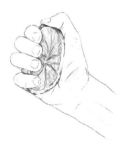

We are
not boxes
Our complexity
cannot be stuffed
inside the spaces
of your small mind
You cannot
stick a label on us

and expect us
to fold and unfold
at your command

– give me the right to
my own narrative

We start writing stories
for ourselves
when we can't bear
the suffering
any longer
Our inner typewriter
takes over
rising

to the occasion

scripting

a fantasy so convincing

that we forget

the reality ever existed

– the story is all i know

The most healing words
are often
the simplest

        – i believe you
        – i am sorry that
           happened to you

Now I know
how the banana feels
after he strips her clothes off
eats her
and tosses her protection
in the trash

– used

It was abuse
and more
It was love
and more

– / com.plex /

(com-plex) adj.
1. consisting of many
   different and
   connected parts
2. denoting or involving
   numbers or quantities
   containing both a real
   and an imaginary part

The sadness
sucks the speech out of me
until asking for support
sounds like
I'm fine

— please help me

Don't ever
promise me anything

– i will believe you

When I awake
you are
someone else
Yesterday's you
is gone
and the only relationship I have
is with change itself

    – we die to each
      other daily

I didn't know
that blood could be so terrifying

– penetration

You are
holding the hope
until I am ready
to take it from you

– thank you

I learned betrayal
the day you promised me I would enjoy it
after I said no

– so you know me better
than i know myself

A hug

was never

just a hug

– when every touch
is sexual

Make me hard
you said
so I sacrificed my innocence
Don't be demanding
you said
so I sacrificed my pleasure
Make sure it doesn't happen again
you said
so I sacrificed my addiction
Don't be angry with me
you said
So I sacrificed my truth

Say you still love me
you said
so I sacrificed my sanity
Marry me
you said
you said
so I sacrificed myself

– you killed me

How is it possible
to lie naked next to someone
without wanting
to disintegrate

– shame

The last time I saw you
you waved
and said see you soon
I have been waiting
for you ever since

– like a soldier's wife

I will
make time for you
and take you out to play
I will reclaim you
as my own
wrap you up in blankets
and hold you
in my arms.
But most of all

I will be
the saviour
you should have had

– inner child

Did I really lose it
Or does it not count
unless I agree to it

– virginity

It meant nothing you said
as tears streamed down my face in the car
But you took everything

– sold

I broke myself
into a million
shattered pieces
so you wouldn't
leave me
and yet
the weight on my shoulders
was lifted
when you did

– the body keeps the score

Where did you learn
that sex is dirty.
who taught you
about sin

        – it must have been
        my fault

You come back to me

at night

to terrorise me

and then you reappear

to comfort me

       – memory is a double-
       edged sword

I will panic
if men get too close
their sudden movements
remind me of a time
when closeness meant death

– i don't deserve to
feel secure

There is nothing
like the fear you feel
when you don't know
you are scared

            – the fairy tale isn't
            making sense

If I was good enough
maybe you wouldn't have hurt me

– *third stage of grief*

I lost my hero
when I lost you
and since then
I have searched for my hero
in unavailable men

– the repetition
compulsion

I make scars
on my body
so that I can feel
the sting
And be reminded
of what is mine

– wounded in battle

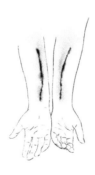

To lose

the man who became

my entire existence

or to lose

my entire existence

– double bind

I needed to be
more than enough
because you
asked that of me
because the world
asked that of me
but not
because I ever wanted to

– perfectionism is unkind

Ending my life
would be
the ultimate freedom
from you

– closure

We learn to let go
of the past
without running away
from the past

— a non-linear process

She's not
going to appear
in some imagined future life
She doesn't come out
only when things have
fallen into place
There's no point waiting
for anything or anyone
to bring her
She's here
And she's been here all along

– finding Me

It was the broken boy
living in you
who broke the little girl
that was me

— i'm sorry i couldn't
fix you

She buries herself in books
searching the pages
for the identity he took

– lost and found

I want to tell you
my story
but the words
don't feel like they have permission to speak

– silenced

I can ride my panic attacks
better than you ever rode me

        – if you could see me now

If I was so in love with you
why did I tell my friends
never to fall in love

    – the soul knows

She has never felt
arms around her
that didn't make their way
inside her

– will you hold me

I wish

you could help me

without me having to say a word

– rescue fantasies

My body is tired
of the part it has had to play
it needs to break down
To be reborn

– rock bottom

I am in awe
of myself
I watch me
Fighting to stay alive
every day
Carrying the kind of pain that
kills people
And I am amazed

— can I be my own
higher power

I didn't need you to say it
I needed you
not to teach me
your version of it

– i love you

Take them away
from between my legs
and put them in handcuffs

– the right to remain silent

I told you
I was sexually abused
and you acted
like I told you
I had picked up food for dinner

– blank faces

Only the surface is visible
no one sees the underneath
what would happen
if the duck stopped paddling

– drowning

In the breaths you take
between sentences
lie my cries
screaming to be heard

– just listen

What crime
did I commit
What did I do to deserve
pain
instead of pleasure
as a punishment for loving you

   – abuse is a life sentence

I couldn't tell you
Because I was told
not to tell you
Because there was nothing to tell
Because I couldn't
tell myself

– i am not a liar

What happens to the fish
after the man hooks it
reels it in
and discards it
How can it be expected
to swim again

  – never be the same

At what point
did God abandon me
Maybe it was
after He gave me
so much to be grateful for
Maybe it was
after He saw me lying in bed
covered in cum and tears
Or maybe it was
after He promised
never to abandon His people

– not my god anymore

Searching through hundreds
of my contacts
knowing
I can't ask any of them for help

– doomscrolling

How did you manage

your twisting and turning and stabbing

deep inside me

holding me down with your weight

and still

making me believe I wasn't trapped

– bruised

There is a part of me
waiting to erupt
from the volcano
of repression
she is banging in the cellar
of a gated castle

　　　　– let depression deliver
　　　　her message

Asking didn't work
pulling away
didn't help
Faking
was the only option

– orgasm

Do you really want to know
how I am
or will you ask the question
and leave
the answer unread

      – teach me how to
        trust you

I was never taught
where I ended
and you began

– blurred boundaries

Let me help you
so that maybe you will notice
that I need help too

– begging

There is no one
hiding in the bushes
no reason
to panic in the dark
the man running past me
is just
running past me

    – everything.
    could.
    kill me

The world
could not keep me safe
maybe heaven
can give me
another chance

– not every cloud has
a silver lining

Five years later and I am an adult
And I have only just learned
that I can say no
whenever I want

   – things they should
     have taught at school

I liked the way your words stung me
Like the lashes
administered for sin
the hurt reminded me
not to stray
from your definition of good enough

– desensitised

Surely the women are to blame
for leading on the men
Didn't you know
that men can't control themselves
when they're aroused

                – yes they bloody can

I became like clay
when you spoke to me
I shifted and moulded myself
so that my opinions
became buried so deep
under your denial of my reality

– gaslighting

There comes a point
when the numbness lifts
and I am strong enough
to jump off the bridge
or strong enough
to rise from the dead

– the choice is only mine

;

The words

that once tortured me

now save me

– He Is Gone

It did not

happen for a reason

I am not

Stronger

because of it

And I definitely

definitely

do not have to forgive him

to move on

— toxic positivity

Why
did I need you
So badly

– hunger

Were modesty

purity

and tradition

really more important lessons to learn

than my right to have a choice

       – who came up with that

       class curriculum

Now
the panic does pass
it can express itself
I don't need to feel its pit of dread
stuck in my body
from the moment I wake

– the worst is over

Because bad things
happen in the dark

– that's why

Living in the moment
would have been fine
If my world
hadn't come crashing down
after the moment

– your philosophy
had consequences

It hurts
Please can this be over
Get off me
I don't want this anymore
and I never wanted it
in the first place

– *internal monologue*

I have finally
reclaimed my anger
and now it is being labelled
A Personality Disorder

— doctor's orders

What words
could I have used
when the only ones I knew
were not enough

– please stop

My small
baby heart
had enough space to
fill itself with you
How come your big
adult heart
didn't do the same for me

– power imbalance

It was you
who played the game
It was you who
made the rules
It was you
who changed them
the second I learned how to play

– checkmate

Of course I wasn't as fun
as the other girls
I was too busy
surviving
to have fun

– childhood

You felt like
a dagger
lodged in my body

      – apparently pain
      is pleasure

It was

not perfect

I think it might have been

problematic

It was misuse

No, abuse

He Raped Me

– searching for the words

I will never forget
the moment
I saw colour again

– medicinal sunsets

After sex
I needed you to take me in your arms
and hold me
whilst tears rolled down my face
I needed you to
tell me
that you loved me
that I was brave
that you were here for me
I just needed you
to do one nice thing
Getting mad at me
was not what I needed

– the aftermath

Reaching for you
across the bed
And watching you
turn away from me

– Jet me in

It didn't end
when he left
It just turned into
a never-ending replay
in my mind

– rape on repeat

You give me this pain
and expect me to cope with it
You drive me to the point
of staring death in the face
and tell me it is part of an all-loving plan
that I have to find meaning in
You say
you are the definition of perfection
that you are
A faithful God
Who does no wrong

– How Dare You

Sometimes we latch ourselves
onto people
hoping they will fill our empty
voids
And we don't realise
that releasing ourselves
is how we fill our empty voids

— unchained melody

She wants to be
the sound a telephone makes
when it's disconnected

– *suicide*

Maybe you flipped me over
and turned me around
because looking me in the eyes
would have told you the truth

– selective blindness

My relationships are like
a jug of water
that gets filled quickly
Filled with the false hope
and reassurance
that the water won't ever leave the jug
But the water does leave the jug

Sometimes suddenly and sometimes
bit by bit
However it happens
I always feel the same

– empty

Please
don't do it
Nothing is
worse
Anything
but that

– the silent treatment

I welcome
the heart-pounding mind-numbing
head-swirling experience
of panic
I let its rhythm symbolise
Victory
from dissociation

– feeling is a sign
of healing

In the spaces between
your abuse
and your bottling of emotions
Were the times you told me
how lost you felt
how tormented you were
how much you were hurting

– that is what i miss

Fearing that you will leave me
Expecting you
to leave me
Knowing
with every part of my anxious
traumatised
broken self
That you will leave me
Is just as painful
as you leaving me

– the grief before the grief

You need to let me go
was the last thing
you demanded I do

– holding on to you is my
final act of disobedience

You are a vessel
of kindness
But kindness is unfamiliar to me
And I don't have the receptors
to receive you

– it takes time to
believe in something
for the first time

I ask her what she wants
and she doesn't know
I ask her what she needs
She says she doesn't really
get asked
that question
She says
She has only ever learned
to meet the needs
of others

– come home to yourself

Then the day
becomes a fog
You could hit me
and I wouldn't feel it

– numbness

I don't want you
to move too far away from me
But I don't think
I can get any closer right now

– relearning intimacy

It is impossible to pray to you
to read your Bible and follow your
traditions
to stand before you
repenting for my sins
knowing
that you betrayed me.
Believe me
I don't want to hate you
I would much rather
stop believing in your existence altogether

– the lord our
righteous saviour

I am lucky to have a house
a big house
Other people say
it's a perfect house
It wasn't his house
But every inch of it
is filled with memories
of how he hurt me
In my house

– homeless in my
own house

She is an adult
who lacks common sense
because when she was
a child
none of her problems could be solved
by using common sense

– like an untrained muscle

Choose the language
you want to speak in
and don't change it
because you are scared

           – your mixed messages
             will hurt me

I wish I could have been

an older sister

for myself

I would have protected me

I would have overprotected me

So that years later

when I sit in therapy

my biggest issue

is that my older sister overprotected me

– if only i could
time travel

It's an ache
that doesn't leave
It's rain
that stays stuck on my lashes
without ever falling down
Shards of glass in my heart
perhaps softer
perhaps more like old wounds

bruising on my chest
It's loneliness
and more loneliness
and it hurts
So badly

– *sadness*

He lives on in me

every time

I can't watch the movie

because there's a rape scene in it

He lives on in me

every time

I can't get the massage

because I'm scared of touch

He lives on in me

every time I look happiness in the eye

and can't feel happiness

– he is immortal

The knowledge that I am
Whole
even when I am made up
of a million broken pieces
That I am
Whole
All by myself

– freedom

When did life as I knew it
really end
It might have been
when life as I knew it
ended
Or it might have been
when I realised
that life as I knew it
had ended

– it happens twice

I've learned that it's about
letting it mean multiple things
But mostly
letting it mean myself
And never
putting it all
into another person

– where's home

Going for months without
eating or
sleeping
or moving
It's like she's trying
To disappear

– slow suicide

Maybe
I'm codependent
Or maybe I've
just lost too many people

      – again and again
      and again

I've dealt
with so many things
on my own

       – i thought i had to

I made it through another year alive

– defying the impossible

Let the flashbacks
rise from your mind
my therapist said
let them fly to this room
and choose a box
to contain them in

– you are safe now

Acknowledgements

This book simply couldn't have been published without a hell of a lot of support. It is not something I would have opened up for the world to see if I didn't have some hardcore allies by my side; friends, family, and loved ones who have each lifted me up in their own individual way, giving me the strength to be the authentic, vulnerable, and raw version of myself, and validating and listening to my experiences without judgment. That also includes the amazing individuals who supported me by reading my work pre-publication: especially in the early stages, my strong conviction that I needed to publish these poems was often intermingled with waves of doubt; hearing your honest opinions helped enormously to clarify my decision. Thank you to all of you for believing in me, for holding space for me, and for hyping me up. Whether by sitting in a restaurant late at night with me, going through poem after poem until the words made me sick and you ordered me a hot chocolate, or enthusiastically reading through my work and giving me feedback at a very stressful time in your own life, or sending me 67 messages at 3am to tell me, "Jemima do not, I repeat DO NOT, take any poems out of the collection"—I appreciate you dearly.

A huge thank you to Right Angles, especially my agents, Hayley Woodward and Mia Hadrill, for being so attentive and encouraging throughout this entire process, and for embracing this project with passion. The fact that you continue to listen to and answer the WhatsApp voice-note-TedTalks I send you every two seconds amazes me—thank you for taking me seriously, whilst reminding me not to take myself so seriously.

Thank you to Amelia Spooner for being a wizard with pastel colours, for the ideas, inspirations and mood-boards, and thank you to Cara

Sheffler and Nikki Muller for your detailed editing. A big thank you to Julliana Lagerstedt for your beautiful illustrations—I genuinely couldn't have asked for better visuals to accompany my poems, and to Sarameeya Aree for your wonderful cover design. Thank you to Sam Pearce at SWATT Books for publishing and typesetting.

Thank you to those who have opened up and shared their personal experiences with me over the years. And thank you to those who continue to speak out—my healing journey would never have begun had I not heard from and read the works of brave individuals, those willing to talk about the difficult things nobody wants to talk about.

To my sister and best friend: thanks for taking all of my shit—I don't for the life of me know how you got so good at it. Thank you for always being a proud supporter of my work, for sharing the many emotions these poems have brought out, and for agreeing to multiple Zoom calls from abroad to discuss every step of this book. I love you.

Lightning Source UK Ltd.
Milton Keynes UK
UKHW020708260822
407840UK00004B/19